food
around the world

Godfrey Hall

Wayland

Titles in this series:
Clothes Around the World
Festivals Around the World
Food Around the World
Houses Around the World
Musical Instruments Around the World
Shops and Markets Around the World
Toys and Games Around the World
Transport Around the World

Title page: Grandad feeding baby using chopsticks, in China.

With thanks to Sue my wife, Hicham Ennami, Mike Theobald, Madeline Murphy, Joan and Harold Vidler.

Series editor: Deb Elliott
Book design: Malcolm Walker
Cover design: Simon Balley

First published in 1995 by
Wayland (Publishers) Limited
61 Western Road, Hove
East Sussex BN3 1JD

British Library Cataloguing in Publication Data
Hall, Godfrey
   Food. – (Around the World Series)
   I. Title II. Series
   641.3
ISBN 0 7502 1247 0

Typeset by Kudos Design Services
Printed and bound by Rotolito Lombarda s.p.a.

Acknowledgements
The publishers would like to thank the following for allowing their pictures to be reproduced in this book: APM 6; Bryan and Cherry Alexander 8; Cephas 11 (bottom, Nigel Blythe), 13 (bottom, Sand Hambrook), 19 (David Copeman), 21 (bottom, Chris Davis), 23 (William Talarowski); Eye Ubiquitous 9 (top, Julia Waterlow), 13 (Jimmy Holmes), 15 (John Miles), 22 (Anthea Beszant), 28 (bottom, Julia Waterlow), 29 (Edward Shaw); Sally and Richard Greenhill 9 (bottom, Sam Greenhill), 27, 28 (top); Godfrey Hall 17 (top); Robert Harding Picture Library 16, 20 (bottom); Impact Photo Library 17 (bottom, Mark Henley); Life File 20 (top, Juliet Highet); Link Picture Library 4 (inset, Eric Meacher), 11 (top); Zul Mukhida 5, 18 (top), 24; Rex Features 12 (inset, Patsy Fagan), 14 (top, Fotex/I. Wandmacher), 21 (Patsy Fagan), 26 (Rick Colls); Tony Stone Worldwide 4 (main, John Callahan), 10, 25 (Nicholas DeVore); Telegraph Colour Library 12 (main); Alison Thomson 22 (bottom); Julia Waterlow contents page; Wayland Picture Library 18 (bottom, Andy Hasson).

Contents

Our food

The food we eat may be grown or made nearby or on the other side of the world.

Rice grows in paddy fields in the Philippines and other parts of Asia.

These delicious sweet biscuits from Italy are made from flour, sugar and almonds. Some are decorated with icing sugar and others are filled with jam.

Breakfast

In Britain breakfast might be cereal or tea and toast. Very hungry people might enjoy fried egg and bacon, mushrooms, tomatoes and sausages.

6

A French breakfast is often just coffee and fresh bread or croissants, bought from the local baker's.

Lunch

The Inuit people live in the cold lands of North America and Greenland. These Inuit girls from Baffin Island are enjoying a lunch of raw seal meat.

Lunch in China may be noodles, eaten with a pair of thin sticks called chopsticks.

Schoolchildren in India may eat rice and a dish made from lentils, such as curry, stew or soup.

Dinner

Pasta was first made in China, many years ago. Now it is popular in lots of other countries, especially Italy. You can get lots of different types of pasta, like spaghetti, fusilli and rigatoni.

A Bushman and his daughter preparing their evening meal of cornmeal mash in Gautcha, Namibia. To make cornmeal mash, fresh corn is pounded to squeeze out the corn starch. It is cooked in boiling water, then mixed with vegetables or dried meat.

In Pakistan dinner often includes bread, yoghurt, chicken or some other type of meat, lentils and rice.

Snacks

In Honduras in Central America, a tasty snack may be a piece of grilled corn.

You can buy tai-yaki at this roadside stall in Tokyo, Japan. Tai-yaki is made in the shape of red snapper fish and is similar to a pancake. Inside is a sauce made from red beans and sugar.

Selling peanuts to hungry passers-by at a market in West Africa.

Sweets

Chocolate bars and wrapped snacks are often eaten to give you extra energy during the day.

Many children like ice-cream, particularly in hot weather. It is made by whipping together cream, sugar and eggs and then freezing the mixture.

This girl lives in the beautiful Amazon rainforest in Brazil. Her favourite type of sweet is rock honey. Honey tastes very sweet because it has its own natural sugar. This means it is much better for us than ordinary sweets, which have lots of white sugar.

Drinks

Tea is a popular drink. In many countries people drink teas made from herbs, such as mint or camomile.

In Jordan, people buy coffee from stalls at the roadside. It is served from large urns.

Fizzy drinks are popular all over the world. However, most fizzy drinks have lots of sugar in them which can rot your teeth.

Bread

A loaf of foccacio bread from northern Italy. It is made with salt and olive oil.

A bread shop in Baden-Baden in Germany. The bread has been baked and put together to look like bulls.

Nan bread is a flat, leaf-shaped bread. In Dubai, it is baked in a very hot stone oven. People like to eat nan bread with fruit and yoghurt.

Fruit

Only the yellow part of Jamaican ackees are eaten.
When they are cooked, they taste a bit like
scrambled eggs.

Rambutans are a popular fruit in South-East Asia.
They are eaten raw.

Oranges are a type of citrus fruit grown in Israel, among other places. Lemons, limes and grapefruit are types of citrus fruit, too.

Coconut is the fruit of the coconut palm tree. The white fruit inside the hard shell tastes delicious. You can drink the coconut milk, too.

21

Vegetables

There are many different types of beans. Runner beans are very popular in England. The whole bean is cut up before it is cooked and eaten.

Onions are used in cooking throughout the world. Some markets in Asia sell several different types of onion.

Pumpkins and corn are popular vegetables in the USA. Pumpkins are also used to make pumpkin pie, which is a sweet pudding.

Herbs and spices

Herbs and spices are used in cooking to add flavour to food.

Lemon grass, kuchai and red chillies are used to make Thai food.

Selling spices at a market in Udaipur in India.
Indian food is famous for its delicious and
interesting spicy flavours.

Celebrating

Children all over the world love birthday parties.
There is often special food, like a cake. This may
have candles on the top, one for each year of the
child's age.

Before a Hindu wedding, there is a ceremony
when the families eat special foods together.
These may include vegetable curries, salads and
special sweet dishes.

Religious foods

At the Diwali festival, Hindus prepare a display of food which they later eat together.

Making tsampa cakes for a festival in Tibet. Tsampa is butter mixed with ground barley in tea.

In Bali in Indonesia, colourful arrangements of food are offered as a gift to the gods.

Glossary

camomile   A herb used to make herbal tea.

cereal   Food made from grain such as wheat and eaten at breakfast.

chopsticks   A pair of thin sticks which many people in Asia use to eat their food.

croissant   A flaky bread roll shaped like a half-moon.

lentils   The seeds of the lentil plant which are cooked and often used in soup or other dishes.

paddy fields   Fields planted with rice.

pinenuts   Nuts from the pine tree.

raisin   A dried grape.

urn   A large pot used for making tea or coffee.

Books to read

The Usborne Book of World Geography (Usborne, 1993)
Food For All Seasons, Saint (Activity Digest)
Middle Eastern Food and Drink, Osborne (Wayland, 1988)
Korean Village, Ashby (A&C Black, 1986)
Focus on India, Husain (Hamish Hamilton, 1986)

More information

Would you like to know about the people and places you have seen in the photographs in this book? If so, read on.

Our food
Rice terrace in Ifuago in the Philippines.
Customer eating at a rice stall in Saigus, Singapore.

Breakfast
A croissant is a flaky, moon-shaped bread roll made of yeast dough similar to puff pastry. It can be eaten on its own, dipped in coffee, or eaten with jam and butter. Fried breakfasts are no longer so popular because fatty or fried food is considered bad for our health.

Lunch
The Inuit diet includes raw seal, whale and reindeer.
Eating noodles in Guiyana, China.
Schoolgirls in India eating lentil stew.

Dinner
Different types of pasta. Spaghetti and spaghetti verdi (green), made with spinach.
Bushmen are members of the hunting and gathering people of southern Africa, especially the Kalahari region.
Shiite Muslims at dinner in Karachi, Pakistan.

Snacks
A cornfield near Portageville in New York state, USA. Corn is eaten as part of a main meal or as a snack.
Snack food stall in Tokyo selling tai-yaki
Peanuts for sale in West Africa.

Sweets
Most people love chocolate. However, too much can add to tooth decay.
Eating ice-cream on a hot summer's day in London.
This girl belongs to the Arara people who live in the Amazon Xingu Basin in Brazil.

Drinks
Herbal teas are considered much better for our health than ordinary tea because they do not contain caffeine.
People will often stop at a roadside stall in Jordan for a cup of coffee.
Fizzy drinks are drunk all over the world. One of the most popular flavours is cola.

Bread
Foccacio bread is traditional to the northern part of Italy.
German bread is often dark with a strong flavour, as it may contain rye flour.
Nan (naan) bread is made using yeast and is baked in a very hot oven.

Fruit
The famous Jamaican ackees are usually eaten with codfish.
Rambutans are grown in South-East Asia. This bright red edible fruit is covered with hairs.
Oranges are grown in warm climates, especially Spain and Israel.
This photograph shows a mother and child eating coconuts as part of a coconut festival held each April on Hainan Island, China.

Vegetables
Close-up of runner beans, sliced and ready for cooking. Runner beans are also known as scarlet runners.
Onions for sale at a market in Vietnam.
Pumpkins and corn for sale outside a shop in Pennsylvania, USA. Large, round pumpkins have a thick orange rind, pulpy flesh and numerous seeds.

Herbs and spices
Herbs and spices used in Thai cooking are widely available in most supermarkets and specialist shops. Popular Thai dishes include kai-tom-kha, which is chicken galingale (herb) in coconut soup, and om-yam-kung, which is a prawn soup.
Indian food is well-known for its use of spices. Different regions of the country have their own methods of cooking and preparing food and use different blends of spices.

Celebrating
Birthday party held in Ealing, west London.
Curries made from vegetables, rice and salads are served at Hindu weddings together with non-alcoholic drinks.

Religious food
Diwali is a Hindu festival of lights when presents are given.
Tsampa cakes are made from butter mixed with ground barley in tea. This photograph was taken in Lhasa, the capital of Tibet.
Offerings of food at a temple near Ubud in Bali, one of the many thousands of islands in the Indonesian archipelago.

Index